This Is What

Real Love

Feels Like

Sylvester McNutt III

Copyright © 2017 Sylvester McNutt III

ISBN: 1540509168
ISBN-13: 9781540509161

The names in all of these stories, poems, and anecdotes have been changed to protect the identities of any person(s) real, exaggerated, or made up. *This Is What Real Love Feels Like* and Sylvester McNutt III are not suggesting or promoting any lifestyle or choices in this book. This book is written as a true expression of art, of poetry, and of creativity. This book is written from the perspective and opinion of the creator, and he reserves the right, at any moment, to change his perception of anything presented. The author, the publisher, or person responsible for delivering you this text is not liable for any undesirable outcome(s).

This Is What Real Love Feels Like
by Sylvester McNutt III

All social media links, contact info, bio,

and tour dates can be found at

www.sylvestermcnutt.net

Artists Credits

Kylie Morgan
@misskyli3 on Instagram
kyli3M0rgan@gmail.com

Saumyaa Mehra
@saumyaamehra on Instagram
saumyaa.mehra@gmail.com

Jamie Dunek
@jamiedunek on Instagram
jamie@jerseymanmagazine.com

Kely Torres
@merakartcollection on Instagram

Saskia Brown
Saskiabrown.9@gmail.com

– Artists, thank you for sharing your art with me, with my readers, and with the universe. Each one of your pieces meant something to me. Keep creating, keep sharing, and never stop the process of creating from your heart.

Contact and Social Media

Contact: slymcnutt@gmail.com

www.sylvestermcnutt.net

Instagram: www.instagram.com/sylvestermcnutt

Youtube: www.youtube.com/slymcnutt

Facebook: Sylvester McNutt III

Twitter: www.twitter.com/sylvestermcnutt

Snapchat: @sylvestermcnutt

LinkedIn: Sylvester McNutt

SECTIONS

WE JUST WANT TO BE LOVED AND ACCEPTED.

– SYLVESTER MCNUTT III

Creation Story

Today is Monday. I started this book about four weeks ago. When I first started writing this project, I had no idea what I was doing, and yes, this is my fifth book. I honestly wasn't sure of the direction I wanted to go with my career. I want to explain. I've been a self-published author for four years. I've sold thousands of books. I've made a name for myself in the field of self-help. I put out a new book every year for the last four years, and each one covered a different topic—topics I thought were necessary for the culture. My first book, *The Accelerated: Success Is a Choice*, is a book I wrote as I was quitting my corporate America job in 2012 and transitioning toward writing full time. *The Dear Queen Journey: A Path to Self-Love* is obvious as to what it's about. This book really launched my name. The third book, *Dear Soul: Love after Pain* is a lot closer to me than anyone will ever know. To make a long, emotional story short, I started writing that book on the day of my father's funeral. I told myself that I knew I was going to experience darkness, sadness, regret, and maybe even a little anger. I told myself that I did not want to stay inside of those emotions too long, so I started writing *Dear Soul*.

I felt like those three books were written in an order that was perfect to precede my masterpiece on dating, *Dear Love Life: Efficient Dating in the Technology Era. Dear Love life* is the most comprehensive, most well-written, and the most objective book I've ever seen on dating. I feel like that book is a straight shooter and just gives fact after fact.

Success, self-love, and then healing before you try to date. That sums up the four books in one sentence. After I healed, launched a successful business, and found myself, then I started dating. It was so much easier to date after a journey of finding myself and healing from my past. It's amazing that as I wrote those books, I felt myself change as a human. I became healthy. I became a person who exuded love. And then I found a woman who I couldn't stop writing about.

After writing some successful books, you do one of two things: you get comfortable, or you create a new one. For months I couldn't figure out what to write. I started seven or eight different projects, but nothing grabbed me. Then magic happened. I was walking into the grocery store with my lady, and I said aloud, "This is what real love feels like." She looked at me like I was crazy, which is standard. It just clicked, like a light switch, that it was time for me to write my perspective on what real love is.

I hope this book can be a pathway for you, a spiritual experience, a fun book that you often times refer back to. If you've lost a love I hope the prose here reminds you that you can find a new one. If you've lost the pieces of yourself that make you whole I hope the poetry here brings you back some love.

" It's not about looking for love from others. Yes, it's nice and we are lucky when it comes. It's more important that we focus on making ourselves feel like love. Once our inner world is love, the outer world will always follow suit. Trust the process and give yourself the love that your soul is craving."

– sylvester mcnutt

Keep your heart open, your spirits free, and keep your mind uncaged. You're not meant to be trapped and blocked into whatever it is *they* want you to be. No, your life is about love— it's about the love that you have to give, and you will only feel free once you give that love out like how a bird sprawls out over the wind. Fly away. Fly to a land of abundance, of love, of joy. You deserve to be there. Always give your love freely.

—*This Is What Real Love Feels Like*

Head versus Heart

does real love exist? is it worth the time to date again.

step one, look within. if you think love is strange, not worth the time, or just a conglomerate of games, then you'll attract that. your head is telling you that based on what you've seen, and that is not accurate. there is so much information that you don't have. there is so much experience that you haven't experienced. there's no way that you can say real love doesn't exists or that it's not real based on what you have experienced. it's inaccurate. your heart knows that real love is already inside of you. your heart knows that the more you amplify that love, the easier it will be to manifest that love all over your life. so to answer your question, yes, real love exists, but you have to believe it. if you don't believe it, then there is no point in continuing this thread. once you're ready to believe it, then you will manifest it every step of the way. so the real question is not you asking me if real love exists. the real question is supposed to come from me to you—do you believe that real love exists?

— Sylvester McNutt III

Your life as you know it is an amalgamation of complexities of your past and seeds of your future. There are tanks outside on the streets shooting bowling balls into the buildings in which your identity lives. You have to allow them to blow up everything. You must deal with the rubble, the broken pieces, the uncertainty. Your heart knows that you care as much as you can, but your brain knows that you care about the wrong things at the wrong time. You're trying to find your center, your calm. You're looking to get back to square one, but that'll never happen. There is no closure coming for you, only change and more uncertainty. Your uncertainty is a result of your desire to control your future, your desire to predict life versus living in the moment.

– Sylvester McNutt III

You're transforming because it's time for you to live. It's time for you to become a higher version of yourself, and you're never going to do that while plotting and scheming. Now is the moment. Now is where everything is happening. You're like that kid on the playground who is stuck between trying to monkey bar between two bars. You're holding on to the one behind you...fear of failure. It is your time to let go and allow yourself to fall if you have to.

– Sylvester McNutt III

Look all around you. All you see is change, transformation, and new life. It's time for you to drink more water, to listen to audiobooks that empower you, to listen to yourself for once, and to connect with the avenues of life that really matter to you. This is a selfish moment, and that is okay—you're done living for society, for your parents, for your spouse. It's your turn to live for you, even if it's just for one day. You're creating a new you, and as a result, this will make everyone's life better. You're losing your mind a little, but that's just a part of the process. Every part of growth has a little bit on uncomfortableness involved. Today, there will be no more head-versus-heart battles. You are one. You are synced. You are in line with yourself and the divine.

—***Transformation***, Sylvester McNutt III

At this point, you don't deserve to
be in empty beds thinking about
people with empty hearts and
broken promises.
Sleeping next to bodies that should
feel like furnaces in the middle of
the summer, and yet they don't. The
connection has faded.
Feeling alone while next to another
is just wrong; your heart didn't sign
up for that.
That's not the love that you really
want to settle for. That's not the
song that you signed up for.
Your heartbeat has more rhythm
and soul than that—it's time to
change the station.

   *—**empty**,* Sylvester McNutt III

Listen to yourself.
Your heart says that
you love a person and
that you have to stay,
but your brain is telling
you that this individual is just a
lesson, just an example of
everything that you don't need.

Are you paying attention, or are you
going to allow someone to destroy
your ability to listen to your own
damn self?
      —*listen*, Sylvester McNutt III

You wish that your heart would listen, but logic doesn't run its course because you feel the craving so deeply, so deeply that your biology changes, and it becomes much easier to shed tears. The tears don't fall because you're sad. No. The tears understand you, and humans don't, so you cry; your heart cries until it fills up oceans. That's not the true battle. The real battle is when you have a fantasy in your head that ruins your present moment, and your reality is skewed and meek because of the fantasies you have created. Maybe they're just the same battle, and we refuse to accept it because we are drunk off of our fantasies after taking shot after shot of potential. Stumbling across words that describe how you feel, but they contradict what you're thinking. How you feel won't change. In fact, it only gets deeper, wider, stranger. You logically want the fantasy to become reality, and until that happens you will crave more, more of what you don't have. The more you crave it, the more suffering you will bring in.

—*C R A V E*, Sylvester McNutt III

Real love: When cell phones go away and the only connection is the silence between each other's heartbeats, the silence that makes each other's souls scream at each other. When two people can look up at the stars, the moon, and talk to each other about everything and nothing. It's a true connection when the only social media presence is each other's voice, each other's thoughts and mannerisms. The only notification needed is when two people can login to each other's servers. A true connection, one built on staring into eyes and not screens, *This Is What Real Love Feels Like.*
　　　　—**true connection**, *Sylvester McNutt III*

I realized that if you have someone who is loyal, who goes hard for you, and who just wants to be a part of your happiness, then you are rich as you stand, right now. In this life, love and time are the only true currencies. Everything else is just made up to control you. Giving love, feeling loved and sharing your time with someone, well that is freeing. That is true abundance and happiness. Becoming rich and famous will show you that it is not the answer. You are wealthy if you have a loyal person, if you have a person who just wants to share moments with you. Money and fame will never compare to having that type of person. That type of love is rare and should be cherished.

—*Real Love*, Sylvester McNutt III

The playing field was never even. Confusion, mixed with another bottle, mixed with broken promises and pain that never really left. The pain was only hidden by small, transparent Band-Aids that never healed anything and nude-colored lipstick. She wanted him, but he was over there in a lane that wasn't operable for her heart. She wanted to veer over there, because she deserved to be loved by not just any man but by a very specific man. She never wanted to leave that man alone, even though it was time for her to move on. She never wanted to see that man hold another woman the way she was supposed to be held by him even though his hands were not meant to hold her heart. He was so far away from her. Both physically and emotionally. Somehow, he warmed her heart and became that much closer to her spirit, to her shadows, to the memories of her past. He was a best friend—hell, even her soul mate—but he wasn't her lover. This is why she didn't operate in ways that made sense to others. She wanted that man to come near, to be the one who would erase all her fears. No other man can ever replace this space. This is why it's so hard for her to move on; he is on a pedestal that she hasn't quite figured out how to break.

　　　—*fly away from him*, Sylvester McNutt III

Love can be like the finicky weather in the Midwest. One day you wake up, and it's shiny, bright. The clouds are nowhere in sight. Then by midafternoon you're looking for the first Uber to the airport because you want to get away, from everything. Then as soon as you pull your phone out, all you can do is think about being with this knucklehead that you love, and the flight away turns into the both of you taking a vacation together.

—*vacation love*

Your feet usually work together when you walk, run, and jump. Your hands work together when you need to clap, to hold your food, or to defend yourself from physical harm. But if you expect your heart and brain to be on the same page all of the time, you will be lost forever. They don't sync up when we want but they will sync up when we need it most.

—*sync*, Sylvester McNutt III

next window, please

No, I'm not ready to "get to know anyone." It sucks because yes, I do want a relationship. I want love—I mean, be honest, and go find me a soul who doesn't. Nobody wants to be alone. I do want someone, but right now, it just doesn't seem realistic for me to put myself out there like that. The heart wants it, and I know it's supposed to. The brain doesn't think it's logical, especially after everything that I've been through. I don't want to get hurt. I don't want to put all of my eggs in one basket just to have the yoke cracked because the user fumbled it. There are plenty of options, but right now, I am just not one of them. I am trying to level up my business, my career, and my health. I do want love, and I know it will find me when the time is right, but today, the answer is this: next window, please, because this one is not open for service.

—This Is What Real Love Feels Like

Nobody wants to be alone, in fact it is a natural part of our desires as a human to desire the presence of others. We all want to feel like we belong with at least one other human, with at least one other person who truly understands us. It's hard to stay alone, because, well, that's just not what being human Is about. It's all about connection, friendship, family, and companionship. We all want to be wanted by someone, and there is nothing wrong with that at all. Having a desire to be wanted is human, it's normal, and is exactly what love is all about.

—***to be wanted***, Sylvester McNutt III

I want to be in love forever with a soul that reciprocates passion like I do, but there is a problem, and well, I don't know if anyone will understand fully.
Right now I'm a little guarded, a little jaded, and most importantly
I'm just not as strong as I know I can be. I need my strength back. I need to forgive a few people and let go of a few things. Once I grow past this point, I will be back. I will bounce back to be the greatest version of love possible. Then I'll be able to offer the highest version of myself. Then I'll be ready to fully give the love that I'm capable of. It's time for me to transform, to shift, and to raise my consciousness. I will be introducing a new me soon.

—*going to transform*, Sylvester McNutt III

Erotic Intelligence

It's not only about looks or status.
For me, intelligence is one of the
biggest factors to attraction, to
sexual desire. A mentally stimulating
intellectual is instantly erotic to me.
I crave to hear your words as you speak
about your passions, your goals, the things
that make you human. The skin is what we
are all introduced to, but the brain will keep
me stimulated; the heart
will tell me about my lover's passions,
desires, and all of the complexities that
make someone alive. Tell me all of the
intricate details that make you, you; that's
sexy. Your intellect will turn me on.
—Sylvester McNutt III

The flesh will fade away as
we age, and that is okay.
Intelligence will
always keep me there past
that point of change. A
connection, where
intelligence is admired, will
always go deeper than skin,
and that is why it is so
damn attractive to me.

—erotic intelligence, part two

If a man only compliments her for her
beauty, for how she walks, and for the way
she dresses, then that man will never really
know her. He will only know a small
representation of who she might be. The
smart man will look within. He will find out
her thoughts on life and on controversial
topics. A smart man will challenge her
intelligence and will make her think.
Secretly, she will fall in love with that type
of man as well.

—erotic intelligence, part three, Sylvester McNutt III

Allow your heart to settle with a man who challenges you, a man who makes you think.
A man who expands your consciousness is a man worth falling in love with over and over.
— Sylvester McNutt III

Heaven & Hell

You'll give yourself *hell* if you compare what you have and don't have to the next person. Comparison leads to an early funeral for the present moment—you'll enable discomfort. Disease. A lack of harmony inside of your brain and heart. An earthquake inside of your veins. You'll compete with people who don't *even know you exist*, and you'll find pain inside of the whole process. It will feel like you're trying to put on a pair of gloves that are full of bleach and razor blades, while standing in the middle of the dessert during a solar eclipse. Give yourself freedom and joy; a sense of *heaven* occurs when you realize that you don't have to compare anything, ever. Convince yourself that you deserve to be there even if you presently don't; self-hypnosis is the goal here. Freedom sets in when you realize that you're perfect just the way you are, and then the living hell that you were putting yourself through starts to vanish.

When you're confused, don't look to the head, because the head is going to overthink and process information inaccurately. Use your heart. Your heart can feel the errors, the mishaps. It can feel when you no longer belong in a situation. You just have to convince your head that your heart is correct. It is.
—*your heart won't lie,* sylvester mcnutt iii

Dear Self,

You don't have to put yourself through hell just to experience heaven.
You don't need pain just to feel love. Happiness and abundance can be appreciated without sadness and scarcity. Trust your intuition to put you in blissful situations – it is usually correct.
– sylvester mcnutt iii

Women are passionate. **Emotional.** Empathic. Lovers. You have the innate ability to love with every cell in your body. Please explain to me why you would listen to your brain when you have an internal conflict. It doesn't make sense at all actually. **Your ability to feel is your superpower.** Your heart is giving you the answer. Stay in tune with yourself.

—*your heart knows*, *Sylvester McNutt III*

Use a little heart,
use a little logic,
figure it out, and
move on quickly
from it so you can
prosper at the highest
possible level. Your
brain and heart are
both correct, allow
them to work in
unison with each other.
They are not separate.
You are one;
you are whole.
—***balance***, Sylvester McNutt III

at the end of the day, your mind will come up with crazy reasons to leave, to break it off, and to walk away from a person who you love with all of your being. your heart will remind you that you love them, and that one reason will dilute the thought of leaving.

—*your heart will lead you*

We seek change, but change is about implementing new behaviors. Behaviors are only sustainable with the right mind-set to go along with new actions.

—*change*, Sylvester McNutt III

The *Love at First Sight* Story

I'm browsing through Instagram, a social network in the 2010 era, one day, and I saw a comment on my most recent post that captured my attention. I don't know why I noticed this comment out of the thousands that I get per week. It was a beautiful picture of a sunset here in Arizona. The background had a contrast of blue, orange, and yellow. Cacti was featured on the lower left of this perspective picture. Camelback Road was the gray vanishing point off into the distance. Two-story, light-brown apartments were on the right, and brown condominiums were on the left. Big, puffy cumulus clouds dominated the foreground. It was one of my finest shots ever. I didn't typically share that kind of media with my fans. I liked to share my words, maybe my food, and just keep my interests private. Nobody really knew that I was addicted to sunsets, the high moon, and watching the sky at night.

Her comment grabbed my attention, in the very same way that her black-and-white profile picture did. "I love Arizona skies."
I looked at the comment, and although it wasn't the most intellectual, shocking, or strange comment, it still caught my eye. Again, I can't

really explain why. The universe just told me to click on her profile. I had never seen her profile before. She had six photos. It was a brand-new account. One of the pictures on her profile is actually one of my most prolific quotes from my book *The Dear Queen Journey*. That book came out circa 2015. It was then that I was humbled professionally. I realized that the quote had a fucking typo. I was talking about *lettting* go. That's right—I spelled "lettting go" as "letting go." I wanted to update the book right away, but I lost the PDF file when my computer crashed. I couldn't fix it. As many times as I've posted it and shared it, and considering that thousands of books have gone out with that singular typo, nobody had ever said a word, and I never noticed it until that day. I was a little embarrassed to say the least. She had a picture of her and her best friend—I think it was taken in Vegas, and she was very cute. I wanted to direct message her, but I didn't really know what to say.

Usually, when you are *known*, you can get away with a weak introductory line. The attention you get makes you more desirable to others. It goes along with the "you want what you can't have" paradox. Because of this, I was a little nervous about messaging her, but I was 100 percent confident. So I messaged her, "Tell me about your soul." It honestly felt genuine to me. It felt like that was what I was supposed to say to her. I sent it and put my phone down. She responded with two long paragraphs. A smile went across my face. I read what felt like a poetry book. She was so intense. Direct. Articulate. Our dialogue went one for two days, consistent flirting, connecting. It felt genuine. My desire to meet her in person grew and grew. Our texting felt normal and unforced, which was hard for me because I was always an inconsistent texter at best. When you're in between writing books, sleeping five hours per night, running a company, and trying to lose your mind in the gym, inconsistency happens. With her it was different. The vibe was different. I wanted to text her. I wanted to be consistent. I wanted to give her the attention that I could, the attention that she wanted. I can't sit here and tell you that she was the only person I entertained at the moment, but her vibe felt like something was going to change inside of me.

I had a phone full of women texting me, but I didn't feel the vibe. For a lot of them, I was their safe haven (someone you can trust until you find your soul mate). I was the friend they needed. I was in a space of solitude and solidarity with my connection to the divine. I was single. I had no desire to get in a relationship. I wanted to move when my lease was up in the summer. I was considering relocating to another state, but I hadn't made my mind up yet. I was just casually dating, connecting with a few souls here and there, and growing my business. It's funny too because I write about relationships, so the common assumption is that I am in one or that I should be in one, since I know so much about them. I help thousands of people with their relationships, yet I was in a space where I truly didn't desire to be in one.

It wasn't that I had been hurt, but there was a girl I'd had my eye on prior to meeting her. She moved from Arizona to Minnesota, and that was the downfall of our connection, but I had really fallen for her. It was a "you want what you can't have" situation. She was just twenty-three, and I was twenty-nine. She was still finding time to impress strangers at the nightclub, with a face full of confusion and dresses too tight for her 34-26-38 frame. I loved her smile, her soft voice, and the way she looked at me. I hated the way she used her body to get attention from other men. Her booty was perfect, and her smile was immaculate. She literally had the perfect Hollywood smile, the curves of a goddess, and the attitude to match. No man could resist her. Plus, she had that innocent-bank-manager-who-gets-robbed vibe. I have always been a confident man—hell, maybe even too confident for my own good. It wasn't insecurity that filled that observation—it was a true sign that the vibe wasn't right. The alignment wasn't right. Although I do speak on women's empowerment and how they shouldn't be chained to anyone's expectations, I do feel like my wife has to be cut from a certain cloth, and that isn't negotiable. I expect there are certain expectations that my wife will have of me. Things that she'll require of me before I can secure a lifelong commitment from her. Again, not everyone's wife, just mine. It was a turn off that this girl was into attracting all of these men just for attention. For ego. For dopamine. Attention that I was dying to give her, but she didn't really want; I was just another fool for her temptation. I wanted to book confirmation codes, split utility bills, and split a baby with her. I was past getting attention from strangers and faking a life to fit in with club people who go absent when the real world kicks in. I wanted a wife.

She wanted attention, and because of that, I took an exit to dating seriously and actually committing to a relationship. I was up front and honest about this to everyone I met that year. So I stopped talking to her after several incidents of her showing me that my value to her wasn't high enough to get some basic respect and communication. That's when I met the Latina; soon after I made a decision to leave a woman who wasn't worthy of my space and energy. It was a meeting of the bosses in my mind and heart: hold on to the old woman and a relationship that wasn't working out, or give it a try with the new girl who had potential. The two women contrasted each other so much. This new girl, even though I had known her only two days, seemed to have the perfect connection to me that I had wanted all along. I'm too smart to fall for the spark alone, so I needed to meet her. I needed to talk to her in person. I wanted to see her mannerisms and hear her laugh. Just about everyone is awesome when you first meet him or her. Then the persons demons come out, and that's when you grab a one-way flight to "please don't call me anymore" land.

I wanted to find out about her demons early, so I told her we were going on a date. I asked her if she was free the following day. She was. I set the plan by telling her that we would meet up the next day at the local bar by my house. I actually had no idea where she lived, but when I gave her the address, she said that it was fine to meet there. I was happy to be going out on a date with this stranger, but she never felt like someone new. She felt like an old acquaintance. I felt like I knew her. I even remember writing this short little poem to her while we were texting back and forth: "All best friends and lovers started off as strangers. Be open minded to our connection because you never know."

It was the night we agreed to meet. Our date started at 6:00 p.m., which was perfect because she was off the following day. I was wearing a tee shirt with a crew neck and a white-and-black pattern on it. I liked it because it made my triceps look good. She wore a pair of high-waist distressed skinny jeans with an olive-green long-sleeve tee. Her hair was red, with a copper tone; her skin was glowing like a full moon. We met in the parking lot, gave each other a hug, and went in. Of course, the first meeting was a chance for me to show her my leadership skills. When we walked in, there was a burgundy sign that said Seat Yourself.

I grabbed her hand and said, "Look. There is a spot open, and there aren't any people over there. Let's go sit over there."

"Okay, let's go," she responded excitedly.

Ironically, her ability to trust me within the first minute and my ability to lead her eventually became the blueprint for our dynamic. It started at that moment in the bar.

The waitress came over and greeted us after we got comfortable. My date ordered a Jameson and ginger ale. I ordered Grey Goose and cranberry. That was my go-to drink. I also ordered us two lemon-drop shots. We immediately dove into communicating with each other. We sat across the table from each other, exchanging laughs and smiles, and flirting without touching each other. Our brains mutually connected with each other from the first conversation as we dove into topics about breakups, about the moon and the stars, about each other's passions, and all of the little intrusive qualities that made each other smile.

I didn't want this night to end. It was too good, like a story written in a romance movie. I invited her to my house after a few hours of drinking. We had several rounds, and I obviously didn't want her to drive under those conditions. It wasn't a far walk to my house, and she thought it was a good idea as well.

As we walked to my house under the Arizona night, everything felt right. We held hands. She laughed at all of my silly jokes, and she trusted me. I had never truly felt this level of trust from a woman before. It scared me, to be honest. I was overthinking it. I was anticipating every next step as we got closer to my house. My heart was beating fast. As we were walking, I heard these words come out of the sky, and it felt like the words went directly down my spine: "I know everything that you're doing, and it's all going to be okay." I heard the words come back up my spine, and this time a cold shiver rippled through my body. I was paralyzed for a moment. I couldn't talk; I couldn't move. We became paralyzed in the moment. She took my energy. It was the most uplifting, paralyzing, and interesting moment that

I'd had all year. I felt the anesthesia from the air rush down my lungs as my organs started to shut down. I felt like I was walking in Miami; my arms were moist. Sweat dripped down my arms like I was playing full-court basketball. "Everything is going to be okay." This voice kept punching me in my ribs as I tried to lead this woman to safety, to the throne that I built for her. My legs started trembling like tremors before an earthquake. I looked above, and a black raven sat on a perch. I didn't recall ever seeing a black raven. The raven watched me as my body jerked and my mind fluttered down this sidewalk. I'd always thought that ravens represented death and decay. I looked at my date to see if she noticed this raven; she didn't. I looked back at the raven, and it was still watching me. I saw the eyes of the raven light up like a candle, and its eyes glowed like molten lava, and a beam of light came out of its eyes. The beam went directly into my eyes, and I fell to the ground. I felt my body shaking, failing, shutting down. You never become aware of your heartbeat until you start to lose it. "Everything is going to be okay."

That was all I heard as I convulsed and vibrated on that dirty sidewalk. The rain came. It was purple, and the clouds were blue, and everything started to make sense. The raven took me to death. I deserved to die in order for me to live for her, so the raven killed me. I lost everything that I was because I found everything I wasn't inside of this woman. I didn't know it, but the raven did, so he killed me. I woke up in her arms at three in the morning. She was smiling and watching something on the television. The fan was blowing on my cool body. I looked up into her eyes and saw the same glow that the raven had. The same eyes that the raven had—she had. She looked down at me, and before she could talk, I said, "Everything is going to be okay." She smiled. I smiled. For the next few minutes not a single word was said. We sat there breathing at the same pace, holding each other like there was no tomorrow. Everything was okay. We didn't listen to our heads. We followed our hearts, and they lead us to each other. Everything...really was...okay.

you know, what they say is very true.
you can spend time with her,
you can try to get her to treat you
right, to show you respect.
it may never happen.
and then, out of nowhere, you can
meet a woman who will treat you right,
will show you love, and will value every
second of your existence.

    —be patient brother, Sylvester McNutt III

If you're patient,
loving, and methodical
in your ways, your love
life will always feature a
person who wants to add
value to your beating heart.

    —h e a r t, Sylvester McNutt III

Love at first sight? It's possible. It happens way more than we think. Two strangers can meet, connect with no force, and can stay in touch forever based off of the energy that occurred between the first meeting. That's love at first sight if you ask me. That's real love. Love means *to have a deep admiration for.* Isn't it possible that you can admire someone from the moment your human bodies are introduced to each other? Isn't that love at first sight? I believe so, so yes it's possible.

—*love at first sight*, Sylvester McNutt III

honestly, never listen to anyone who doesn't believe in love at first sight. they'll make the process of being together, of expressing love, and of experiencing each other painful. it is supposed to be a powerful and organic meeting where energy bounces around like the sunlight of the pavement. our little human minds can't control or predict when love is going to strike; we mustn't be such cocky beings. love can happen at any moment, at any time, and in any place regardless of what we think. it's truly not up to you or them to control and predict how or when it will happen—it's up to the vibes.

—*love at first sight*, Sylvester McNutt III

Never stay hung up on someone
who proves over and over that
you're not valuable to them,
that you're not worth their time,
and that your connection to them
is just optional. It might hurt to
leave, but it'll hurt even more if
you stay in a situation that doesn't
feel like home. It should never feel
like someone is laughing at you as
you sit on the edge of a cliff.

—***know your worth***, Sylvester McNutt III

At all times, you can invite new
levels of love into your life.
Be willing to try, willing to listen
to your heart, be willing to be hurt
again, and be willing to give everything
that you have to another person.
If you want the love that we know
you're deserving of always stay willing.
Be willing to sit on the phone for an hour,
to send long text messages or e-mails, and
most importantly be willing to put another
person before you. This is what real love
feels like. Be willing to give it another chance.
Be willing to fly across the country, to walk
miles and miles just for this little
thing we call, love.

   —*be willing*, Sylvester McNutt III

We don't fear falling in love. We fear falling in love and then watching it leave. The true fear is sitting at your kitchen table in your pajamas as you try to pick up the pieces of your broken heart. The pieces that they promised you would never be broken. We fear the people who come in, use our benefits as they need and then leave us there like we never really mattered. We fear fake love, the love that seems so real but it never was.

—*fear of fake love,* Sylvester McNutt III

You should have fear when you find someone new. It's normal. Embrace it. Don't make your potential lover suffer because someone in your past hurt you. Accept the fear, but understand that it doesn't have to control your ability to love again.

—*love over fear*, Sylvester McNutt III

The real fear is that a failed relationship will push you to resentment, to jadedness, to pain. The real fear is that a failed relationship will cause you to lose your sense of self, your happiness, and that you may not be able to recover from the pain.

That's why we avoid love, because in every situation, this is a possibility. If you remember that, remember that love can always lead to harmony, to trust, to a lifelong connection and partnership.

Truth: real love will never scare you or me; traveling to a destination that looks like love just to find out that it is not, well that's the part that nightmares are made of.

—***real fear***, Sylvester McNutt III

If you've experienced any version of love that felt like a steel rod was laying on your forearm in the middle of the summer, as the metal slowly bonded with your skin, searing the flesh second by second, *then* you're supposed to fear the idea of falling in love. Fear and pain are both temporary places of existence, and real love is a force so powerful that it will heal the broken pieces of a heart, will abolish the question marks that end sentences, and will make you have memory loss where past pain existed. Your fear is real. However, know, accept, and understand that it will subside.

—***It Will Pass,*** Sylvester McNutt III

He grew tired of living in this mad world that is full of war and deceit. So he found a woman who understood the things that he understood, and she became his peace. He found a woman who laughed at his jokes and made her own. He loved her because she accepted who he was and then helped him grow into who he wanted to become. All she wanted to do was see him happy, see him smile. He wanted the same things for her. He retired from his previous life to mold a new one with her.

— Sylvester McNutt III

You Deserve More

When things start to click, everything that used to confuse you starts to make sense. You don't feel the urge to question it because you've already attracted and accepted a new direction of your life. Things just aren't what they used to be for you because you're walking away from burnt opportunities that singed your happiness. Everything about you has grown: your emotional awareness, your spirituality, your belief in self. Your life has transformed. You've accepted that you deserve more than what you were used to, and that is why this transformation feels so damn good now. You can literally feel a new you being born. Allow the new energy, the new vibes to flow through you and provide abundance for you and yours. Allow the new mind-sets, the new behavior, the new freedom to guide you. There is a new you, and your growth is so damn beautiful.

—*there is a new you*, Sylvester McNutt III

Takers only know how to take and take. Givers have to learn how to say no, how to not feel bad for saying no, and most importantly, givers have to set some healthy boundaries.

—*g i v e r s*, Sylvester McNutt III

You're a giver. You give everything that you have, especially if you know that others do not have funds, or love, or even something so simple like attention. You'll give your care and concern because you have a big heart like that. You'll stand in line with someone just so that person won't feel alone. You'll sit on the other end of the phone as you feel tears and confusion come into your friend or lover. If we put pictures next to words in the dictionary, *giver* would bear your face and would describe you in its entirety. You're a giver, and all givers want one thing: to be appreciated.

—*the giver's creed*, Sylvester McNutt III

too little, too late, too bad

I had to walk away from you.
It wasn't because I didn't love you.
I did—I mean, I do. It's still present.
It's still here with me now.
The love I have for you will never die.
Even when I do, it'll still be floating around
on this earth, looking to inhabit another person.
I embraced you. The arms of a stranger,
I still remember your touch, but it wasn't good
enough. It wasn't long enough. It wasn't meant
for me. Your touch was meant for another.
I tried. You tried. You cried. I cried.
We cried, and we walked away because
like you said, "It is what it is."
Whatever "it is," that means we cannot be,
and that's not an insult or fallacy.
It's just the dark truth of our path.
We were both too little, too late,
and not enough for each other.
I hope you find the love you deserve,
the love you desire, because I can no
longer offer it to you from this physical
body of mine—I just can't.
I know I will find it too

—Sylvester McNutt III

YOU'LL SEND AN "I MISS YOU" TEXT. MY RESPONSE:

Of course you miss me. You're supposed to. I designed my love like that. **My love is the love that makes you feel like you're the star of a Hollywood movie**, because I will look up to YOU. I do empower. I do uplift my lover. Yes, I had you on a pedestal—you deserved to be that high at that moment. Is my love perfect? No. However, my love is that cold glass of water on a hot summer day that helps you break the feeling of exhaustion and dehydration. You knew I would always have your back, and that is why **I put up with things you knew I didn't deserve.** You were supposed to keep that pain, that trauma, that nonsense away from my heart. You didn't, and that is why I am in a different lane, living. You do miss me. You're supposed to. You miss what I used to do for you. How I'd make you feel. But at this point, you've lost the chances that were given to you, and now I have to choose a different side. At this point, I just deserve more.

—Sylvester McNutt III, *This Is What Real Love Feels Like*

right number, wrong person

You'll call me. You'll text. You'll try to reach out for whatever reason. Maybe you miss me. Maybe you think we can work it out. The time that I'll spend pondering what you want, what it could be, or anything related to you just doesn't exist anymore.

I went back several times, and now I realize something much more important. I realize that my brain is telling me that I deserve more. I deserve not to deal with anyone who wants to break down my happiness. Life is too damn valuable and precious. I just deserve more. Therefore, I have to choose myself. You're calling the right number, but I'm just the wrong person you're trying to reach. You killed the old me, and you don't deserve a chance at the next version of me...
—Sylvester McNutt III

You don't really know me, this new version of me. I've grown. I've matured. I've lost a lot. I have transformed who I am. This process is still occurring, I'm still growing, still learning, & still loving.

Toxic people don't understand just how deadly their behaviors are to their prey. That's why you have to cut it off as soon as it starts. If you don't, it will get stranger, deeper, and will start to feel normal. You'll start making excuses for the pain, and believe me—that's not love. That's control and manipulation. You're done with that. You're not going to be prey for people who are absorbed in the quest to control you or to keep you in a place underneath them.

—Sylvester McNutt III

You Don't Belong

Everyone wants to fit in with everyone else's idea of what everyone else is thinking, and that's the paradox of it all because most people aren't thinking, so people are falling into a trap of mimicking, acting, or thinking in a way like others, who aren't actually thinking. It's called the blind leading the blind.

Everyone wants to follow a trend, but then we laugh at those who are bold enough to go against the grain. Where is the solace in being a follower, sheep, a troll?

We needed to be reminded that it is okay to go against the grain and to live your life in a way that truly makes you happy. In some situations you'll have to accept that you don't belong, and that doesn't make you less worthy. It means that you're a leader, a standout, the one who is supposed to withstand the harsh words of people who can't think for themselves.

I don't block ex friends,
coworkers, or my exes.
You can come see the
struggles, the journey,
& the victories.
I wasn't perfect when
you knew me and I'm not
now, but I will go hard.
I will manifest. I will
overcome. I will love
myself. I will stay true to
myself, to the process of
loving myself and others.

– sylvester mcnutt

Always remember this:
the people who criticize
you for being different
from them are actually
scared to be themselves.
They wish they could live
As comfortable, in their
own skin they way that you
do it. They wish they had
your confidence and ability.
What you may call hate is
really just confused love.
They're on a search for an
identity of their own.
-sylvester mcnutt

you tried it their way—fuck that.

they won't box you into the little boxes
that they live in. you're not a square.
your mind is fluid. it's liquid.
it's dangerous. potent. sharp.

don't let them tell you what you can't
do just because they can't do anything.
that is egregious, and you shouldn't stand
for it. not today. not tomorrow.

never, ever, ever will i allow them
to box you in. your mental capacity cannot
be contained by the lack of theirs.

no. you're a creative, an artist, an
intellectual, a freethinker, a rabbit-hole
explorer. you're awake. you're conscious.
you think outside of the boxes.
— Sylvester McNutt III

Six girls are at the beach near me,
none of them talking to each
other, and there is nothing but
separation between them.
All of them, trapped on the
cell phone. **Is this what the
generation has come to?**

Moments of connection,
of joy, of togetherness lost
to the cell phone.

Lost to the wave of nothingness
that is the rabbit hole of
the Internet, the abyss of
mindless scrolling, and the
shadows of ignoring true
connection just to feel
semiconnected to strangers.

**I ask my generation, what
are we doing?**
— Sylvester McNutt III

It doesn't take much to call and say, "I didn't want anything. I just wanted to hear your voice." That type of treatment can go a long way in connecting with others. Many of us in this generation are stuck in the lanes of working, texting, & scrolling social media. Hold yourself accountable and use the device to strengthen your bonds with humans. Call first, call back, & always practice the art of conversation and connection.

—*c o n n e c t,* Sylvester McNutt III

Allegedly, we live in the generation of connectedness, but is that a sales pitch we are willing to buy? I see people who can't even enjoy a walk in the park or a dinner with their spouse, and they can't sit through a simple class without checking their cell phone. Are we cursed? Are we all addicted to scrolling our devices? Is that true connectedness? Let's be honest—we love social media and text messaging because it allows us to connect right away with other people. There is no shame in that, but there's something much stranger happening. We are allowing the attention from these people to keep us out of accepting ourselves as we are. Snapchat is keeping girls away from engaging in conversation with men at neighborhood bars, and men are losing their ability to commit because finding a date is like shopping for shoes online. I'm not against connectedness. In fact, I believe a certain acceptance of each other is necessary. Living together in harmony sounds good—let's just get back to the basics. Let's make sure we connect when we are supposed to.

— Sylvester McNutt III

Everyone is so focused on acting savage,
busy, and heartless these days. Meanwhile,
I'm searching for the humans that believe
in compassion, love, and human connection.
  —*i am a human*, Sylvester McNutt III

I deserve to attract people who care about love, who care about communicating when there is a problem, and who don't need to wake up just to impress social media or losers that they'll never know. I deserve to bake cookies, to travel, and to experience new memories with a lover who wants to enjoy life, just like I do. I can't act is if I'm some perfect person, because I am far from that. However, I do have so much to give, and well, that's all I want to do. Receive love and give love. This generation will never make me feel strange for wanting something that is so damn human.

—Sylvester McNutt III, *This Is What Real Love Feels Like*

damn, you live in a generation full of people who brag about being coldhearted, who love cutting people off, and whose main skill is allowing friendships to fade away. you don't want to be like the rest of this generation, and you're not going to either. you believe in something much deeper than that.

—*fade away*, Sylvester McNutt III

Honestly, you have to keep asking yourself what you deserve. You might know today, but you can't stop questioning yourself. There are things that you need to let go of: mindsets, behaviors, and even some people. There are new skills that you'll need, new experiences that you'll have to get. You might not be ready for everything that you deserve, but you do have to first ask yourself what you want. Second, you have to put it out into the universe, and last, you have to believe that you deserve it. Believing also means acting upon it. If you never take action, you'll never create what you desire.

— *finding your path,* Sylvester McNutt III

Every single time that you don't take an attempt to advance your brand, that you don't ask the girl or guy out on a date, or you give up being the best worker that you can be you are literally giving YOUR opportunity to another person. Every time that you make excuses and skip the gym, you don't call and check up on friends, or procrastinate with your homework you're GIVING away your opportunity. Nobody cares to hear you complain. Nobody cares to hear that you missed quota. Nobody cares that you missed a workout. The only thing people care about in this world is two things: what you do and how you do it. I command you to be proactive, be the first one there, to show your true skill, to take every shot that you can, and most importantly never fail because of weak effort.

—*e f f o r t*, Sylvester McNutt III

Oftentimes people don't really get you. It takes time for you to build friendships, and some think that you're hiding or being fake, when in fact it's the opposite, because you are so real and transparent that sometimes people literally are lost in the process of trying to understand you. You're the type of person who takes some getting used to. For now, you're just a misunderstood soul, and that is okay. It's not a problem. It really is okay. You cling on to friendships that actually matter. It means you'll adore those who do get to know you. You'll live a victorious life because you won't settle for just any type of connection—you'll settle for connections that spark and ignite something inside of you. Those who understand, those who get you, will get your highest moods and intricacies. Those who get you will never have confusion, nor will they misunderstand your energy.

— ***misunderstood,*** Sylvester McNutt III

The hardest part of it all was trying to explain parts of yourself to people who really didn't even try to understand you. How do you explain to others that you want to be friendly and meet new people but at the same time, you love your solitude? You're like a hit song because you want everyone to know the lyrics to you, but you don't think they'll understand the pain you experienced, which generated the hook, the chorus, and the verses. In a world full of judgment, all you want to do is to find acceptance within yourself. You want to be valued for who you are, today, and not for who you might be in the future. You're a little misunderstood because people don't dance as much as they used to. All you want to do is feel alive, feel worthy, and dance into the night. One day they'll get you, but today, you might be misunderstood.

— ***misunderstood***, Sylvester McNutt III

She doesn't need to be understood. She just needs to be loved and accepted. Love and acceptance is actually a representation of understanding someone—at least, to her it is.

—loved & accepted, Sylvester McNutt III

For so long, I battled myself, I beat myself up verbally, and I never truly lived in a space of acceptance. This is a testimony, a moment of cleansing, something real. Something from my heart, from my story. As tears run down my face like my sideburns, I can tell you that I'm truly happy, truly aware, truly living in abundance, truly living high. But how? Everyone wants to be happy, allegedly, from what I've been told.

An unhappy person who doesn't live in constant bliss like I do is going to ask me how. If me from ten years ago could ask me now how, he would scream at the top of his lungs, "How?" The answer is so profound, yet it is so simple. In fact, you may have heard this before, and I hope you have. I hope that I am not introducing you to anything new. And that's the power of true enlightenment. You're not learning anything new with enlightenment—no, you're literally just shining the brightest light on a pillar of knowledge that will transform your life because you have allowed it to be dim, consciously or unconsciously. That pillar of light is already inside of you. It already motivates you, and you may not even know it. You are the light that is shining on this perspective: **in order to give yourself bliss, you must accept yourself as you are in every moment, without judgment.** No matter the outcome, you reach bliss once you can do that. This is a law of self-acceptance. Accept yourself, and you will elevate yourself. The true power to evolve is right there inside of you, but you have to believe, you have to stop fighting what is, and you must accept yourself as you are in this moment. *This Is What Real Love Feels Like.*

on how to achieve
internal happiness:

you must accept
yourself as you are
in every moment,
without judgment.
—sylvester mcnutt

Never force it. Nothing of value requires an extreme amount of force. Let it flow. Let it be natural. Each day will bring you a multitude of stress, of conflict, and thoughts that will cause you to reflect on possible choices. Don't let the stress or conflict stay. Breathe. Gather facts. Discern the best choices and believe in it. You can be the *conflict*, or you can be the *solution*— either is a choice.

—Sylvester McNutt III

Let go of whatever is telling you to press for conflict because it is unnecessary and unneeded. The only thing that is needed is more love, more understanding, & more listening.

—*let go*, Sylvester McNutt III

happiness is not a destination.

happiness is a reflection of perception, of the present moment, and is only based on what you perceive. to enable happiness, never pursue it. it will always avoid you if you chase something that is actually inside of you. happiness is inside—sit down, pause, breathe, sit in this moment, and allow it to pulsate through you. happiness is never in the past. it's never in the future. it is only in this moment. be still, don't chase anything, don't think about wanting or needing anything. you're not your bank account, your status, or your degree. those man-made achievements will not make you happy. happiness is literally the ability to sit in the moment and appreciate yourself as you are. that's real love. that's happiness.

—*h a p p i n e s s*, Sylvester McNutt III

Most of the time the stress is not even worth it. Consistently remind yourself to let go of things, of situations, and the identity of certain emotions that are truly irrelevant. Certain emotions just sit around inside your heart and linger. They penetrate every level of happiness as if they're on a terrorist seek-and-destroy mission. It's only pain if you allow everything to control you. Breathe. Exhale. Be kind to others and yourself by letting things go.

— Sylvester McNutt III

LET GO OF THINGS THAT ARE IRRELEVANT

Tonight this gentleman ran into me with his cart here at Publix (grocery store in Miami). It happened in the blink of an eye. I felt the metal from the cart dig into my shin. Pain set in. I could've been seriously injured. Initially, anger set in because from my lens, it felt like his neglect and lack of awareness was an attack on my well-being (ego). Objectively, it wasn't what I thought, but I was only able to see that because I have been training for years to view things objectively (removing the ego). It was just someone who literally made a mistake. A mistake. A mistake. A mistake that anyone could make in any grocery store across the country. Whether he apologized or not is irrelevant. We can't wait for apologies that we may never get. There is no power in doing that. We have to be proactive and take charge of our reactions.

I took a mental breath to pause the initial anger that was setting in. That deep breath was to bring mental clarity to myself, and then I walked away because nothing else needed to be done in that moment. No, I don't have to tell him about himself. I don't need to tell him to be more careful. I don't need to victimize myself and complain to him about how he could've hurt me.

He is an adult. He is aware, and even if he isn't, I cannot control another human, ever. This is what I want you to get from this story. Stop picking arguments with people over things that are truly irrelevant.

Then I took a deep physical breath when I was alone. I do this ten to twenty-five times per day. Why? Because *most* of the things that we get angry about are irrelevant. We truly have to remove our self-serving ego and entitlement. Let go of the things that are irrelevant. Please. Do it for yourself. Emotions are a normal part of human existence, but they don't have to control you, not today, not ever.

relationships that work in an efficient way require both parties to practice the art of letting go of things that are truly irrelevant. if you do not, you will be haunted by petty conversations, distractions, and misunderstandings. speak and move from a place a love at all times in your relationship; drop off the baggage of yesterday's argument. it has no place in today's business.

— *l o v e*, Sylvester McNutt III

Living In the Moment **A Short Story**

I was on vacation. It was coming to an end. I wanted to completely be "in the now" and "in the moment" for the last two days of my trip. I didn't ignore my significant other, but I didn't reach out and communicate as often as I had done most of the trip. We would usually talk multiple times a day, which is something we both desired because of the distance. We both have been abandoned by people before, and for us, true love is about communication and attention. We give each other that high-school-love kind of attention. However, the last two days of my trip felt like I needed to immerse myself in the moment. I wanted to appreciate the beach, the sun, and my experience. I stayed off my phone. I was in the moment everywhere I went. I talked to my friends who were around me about the power of staying in the now.

"You have to stay here because there is no happiness in the future; there is no happiness in the past. Stay here," I said to Roger as he played with his cell phone.

"Immerse yourself in the moment. Everything in that cell phone will still be there when you pick it up later, so stay present. There are no emergencies happening right now. Put the phone down and be here. Be totally here," I told him.

The excitement started to rattle through my voice as my octaves rose like the sun over the Atlantic Ocean.

He wasn't exactly sure about the *how* aspect because he had never done it, so I led by example. I sat there still, with my eyes closed, my palms face up, and a smile on my face. I envisioned myself in a happy place, which was physically where I was at. I told him what I was telling myself.

"Nothing else matters. The only thing that matters here is now. If you think about the past, please understand that the past is nothing but dead space, dead time. It's not really real anymore. The past is literally just a story. A story that can have the ability to impact you today, but it doesn't have to, sir. The past is simply the past. Allow it to be there. There is nothing in the future because, honestly, you may not have a future. We don't know what's happening in the future, but we do know exactly what is happening now. Can you tell me what is happening now?"

He was unsure how to answer the question because the idea of meditation or staying in the moment is largely lost to many of us. We sit on our devices, we sit in offices, and we live such busy lives that we neglect the power of sitting in the now and doing nothing. After a few moments of stillness and no reply, I simply told him what was happening with me.

"Sir, nothing is happening, and that is everything. For me, I don't feel the need to be anywhere. I don't feel the need to go anywhere. I don't feel the need to be anything. I don't feel the need to change the music that is playing. All I want to do is stay here, in this moment, because this present moment is the only one that will give me happiness. We are talking. I have no desire to distract myself with the cell phone while we are engaged in conversation. I want to be fully immersed in the conversations with you, sir."

I challenged him to find a similar stillness. Most people don't find it because they don't realize that doing nothing is an option. We are told to be this, to go here, and to rush to this project. All of this rushing causes us to miss life, to miss happiness. We sat there in the moment for what felt like days, and we enjoyed the ambience of the music, the stillness of each other, and most importantly, the happiness that ensued.

For the next forty-eight hours, I stayed off of my phone and looked up instead of down. I went on it now and then: to check the local map, to check my bank account, and to check into my flight. However, I had no desire to talk to anyone who wasn't with me. I spent the previous five days speaking to my significant other every night, telling her how excited I was to see her in the future. Yes, this is fair, and this is normal, but it removes you from the now. By expressing my excitement for the future, she felt valued, and she deserves that from me. She deserves to know that she is valuable and that I am so grateful to share time with her. I also deserve to live in the now and truly appreciate the last moment of my vacation. I fell into a trance that captivated me. There is nothing wrong with finding peace and calmness inside of yourself. In fact, I implore you to. Live in the now.

Here's the funny part about relationships:

all relationships eventually fall into a pattern, and once someone breaks the pattern, it has the potential to cause conflict. People start to question motives, behavior, and the outcomes simply because the pattern was ~~broken~~.

This is why people preach that they want consistency. They don't want to deal with that broken pattern because it's **uncomfortable.** A broken pattern doesn't signify that the relationship is broken, that someone is cheating, or that it will fail. Broken patterns create change, and change is wonderful; embrace it. Adapt. Be open to adaptation as the relationship grows.

—Sylvester McNutt III

Never allow your ~~ego~~,
your ~~pride~~, or a simple
misunderstanding
to keep you away from the
happiness that can and should
live between you and your
partner; don't practice the art
of holding space that breeds
that kind of negativity.

—*ego kills everything*, Sylvester McNutt III

I'm not cold, I just look at people differently once I learn to live without them. They had their chance to stay, and they choose to live over there, away from me, and that choice is theirs to deal with. My only real option is to stay here and figure out how to build my life up. The warmest thing I can do for myself is give to myself, give to my passions, and most importantly continue to give to people who want to be here. People who respect this space and energy.

— *VOIDS*, Sylvester McNutt III

I realized that I had the power one day, and it was magical. There was a time when other people's opinions and thoughts impacted me in a negative way. They caused me to second-guess myself, to put myself at a level much lower than where I should've been. The hateful comments that they gave me destroyed my inner peace and perception of self back then. One day I received a message, and it told me that the only reason others send you negativity is because they aren't complete within themselves. It's because they are weak, empty, and in pain themselves. A person full of love will only offer love, and a person full of hate will offer hate. That is the message I received, and now I'm giving it to you. This is the message that helped me obtain a new level of power. Now, I smile when I'm shown hate, because I refuse to allow it to destroy me. I smile because those people sending hate need to see a smile. They need a representation of happiness, and it is my job to be that. When people say things bad about me I know that it is because they are hurting and I have awakened to a space of peace and love. I want everyone to be okay, to have abundance.

—*awakening*, Sylvester McNutt III

It's so freeing to wake up next to
a person who loves and cares
about you; to be loved
is an immaculate blessing.
Smile at the soul who chooses
yours day after night, and night
after day. Hold her like she's the
last gallon of water on the planet;
cherish the moments you have with
them her and be appreciative of each word
that is spoken.

   —*cherish*, Sylvester McNutt III

You only live _one time_,
so take every risk that you
can to show that girl that
she is more than life.
Hold her tight and breathe
slowly as your eyes gaze into
hers. Allow her to feel that you're
in the moment with her, with
life, with the connection between
the two of you.

—Sylvester McNutt III

She was born to be a lover,
to make other people's lives
better, and to chase sunsets.
Every time the sun falls in the
western sky, she becomes alive
just a little bit more. She smiles
at the possibilities of living to
see another day with people she
loves, people she cherishes.
She yearns for the nighttime
because it is the time of
connection, the time to love.
—*born to be a lover,* Sylvester McNutt III

He was born to be a lover.
As his spirituality rose,
as his appreciation for life
increased, and as his desire
to go through a radical
inner transformation
increased, his desire to
have his queen also
grew. It grew at a rate
faster than the speed of
light. All he wants is to
get a woman who understands
him. A woman who loves him.
A woman whom he can give
everything to.
—*born to be a lover*, Sylvester McNutt III

When you fall in love, everything is different. You think about her needs; you want her to have the time of her life. Love consumes you. She consumes you. You both become each other. *When you fall in love, you* start to do things that you would've never thought of before. Vengeance and revenge leave your heart as you only seek peace and appreciation. You enable a transformative shift in consciousness as your mind goes from me to us, and everything about your life becomes about the entity of you both. Real love is encompassing, and takes over the me. It surpasses the ego, because love is never about ego. It us about the entity that you two have created.

 —*love has no ego*, Sylvester McNutt III

If you're going to fall in love, you might as well fall in love with your best friend. Otherwise, you'll just be creating memories with a stranger. That's the crazy thing about it all. All best friends and lovers started off as strangers.

—*This Is What Real Love Feels Like,* Sylvester McNutt III

Fall in Love with Your Best Friend

My lover has to be my best friend.
I don't want to be in a relationship
with someone I don't even know.
I want us to know each other's favorite
songs, each other's passions, and
the things that boil each other's skin.
There are a lot of empty things in this
world, but a real friendship with my
lover won't be one of them. I refuse to
settle for just sex, just someone to sleep
with, and just a title. I want the bond. I
want the connection. I want the
reciprocity. I want it back, and I'm not
crazy for the desire either. I'm willing
to put the work in for what I deserve.
   —***lover & best friend***, Sylvester McNutt III

I asked her what was wrong. Of course, she said, "Nothing." I'm her friend. I know her better than she knows herself. Then she confessed. She's tired of settling for men who are only part-time lovers, men who truly don't value her. I told her this: "Honestly, you have the total package. You're funny, driven, and extremely attractive. To me, you can get any guy you want. You're settling for less because that's what you're used to. You might be scared of the real commitment because of your past." She went silent. She thought. I was silent. I could hear her soul yelling the words that she so needed to hear: YOU DESERVE MORE. And now the rest of her life will change because she's realized that she has to set her bar higher for the type of man she desires. She is ascending. She is growing into the person she wants to be, and it's so damn beautiful to watch a woman like her blossom. If you get confused or lost, or maybe you give the wrong men an opportunity to your space, come back to the climb, to the ascension.

    —she is ascending, and it's beautiful,
        Sylvester McNutt III

A woman like her deserves
to feel the full-fledged force of
another's love. Not because of
some self-righteous feeling.
Simply because she loves as
if every day is the last day.
Simply because she is willing
to give everything she has to
those she cares about.
She will put herself in the line
of fire to protect her lover, her
children. She wants to learn
her lover so they can grow,
so they can prosper. Any woman
who is willing to give it all deserves
it all too.

—***a complete lover***, Sylvester McNutt III

The Love She Deserved

She deserved the type of love that hit her so hard it made her love herself more, the kind of love that made her stop second-guessing herself, and the kind of love that validated all of her simple complexities.

She deserved to be loved for all of the little broken pieces that she has healed, for all of the tears that she gave to people who didn't deserve her energy. She is a go-above-and-beyond type of lover. She is ready for her lover to reach into her heart, to wrap his hands around it, and to pump it every few seconds, giving it life while looking her in the eyes.

She's ready for a lover who is literally life, literally a reflection of the divine, a lover who literally has the power to heal and grow her. She deserves a lover who is a healer, a nurturer, a leader, and one that understands her. *This Is What Real Love Feels Like...*

—Sylvester McNutt III

You know what really makes a man
fall in love? I'll tell you. See, these
societies put so much pressure on
men to be strong, to be leaders, and
to always be sure of every choice that
we make. Well, as a man, we secretly
fall in love with the woman who allows
us to be truest to who we are; it's easy to love her.
We don't like being forced to live
up to expectations of what a "real
man" is because we are all different.
We want our woman to look
at us, accept us, and acknowledge that
she thinks we are man enough for her.
A real man wants to be accepted,
he wants to be loved and respected,
and he wants a woman who supports
him to grow at his pace.
  —***he wants to be accepted***, Sylvester McNutt III

Yes, you're right. I am a
little broken. I am a
little scarred from what
I've been through.
I still want to be loved,
and well, I don't think
there is anything wrong
with that, do you?
—*a question*, Sylvester McNutt III

People want to post about their "relationship goals." They want to brag publicly about how another person treats them. We can be honest—it's an amazing feeling to know that you have someone who treats you well, who cherishes you, but I guess I'm different. I don't really want to post about it often, as if it's a duty or task. I want to be in the moment and appreciate the moments. I keep it private to a degree. I keep it close to my heart because that's where it belongs. My relationship goal is to always respect and cherish the connection. That's just the type of person I am. I care about our connection, our bond. I care less about what other people think about it.

—you keep it private, but it's real, Sylvester McNutt III

Deeper *in Love with Her* A Short Story

The weather was starting to break in Arizona. This summer was hot, usually in the triple digits, but it didn't burn my skin like other summers. The clear skies make it easy for the sun to touch every inch of the land, like a kid in a grocery store who veers away from the cart.

This was one of the best summers I'd had in a long time. I dated a girl I genuinely liked, and for the first time in a long time, a girl who actually understood what I understood about life. It was beyond her understanding that made me attracted to her, beyond me liking her presence. I loved her; she was the missing piece to my life that I've been hoping for. I'm trying to think back on what life was like before I met her, and it's really blurry, really gray.

For my birthday, she got us tickets to go see pop star Drake and rapper Future. I was a fan of both; so was she. We both enjoyed the same music. We introduced each other to new music. It's a type of connection you couldn't create in a comic book or love novel even if you tried. It was too pure and organic with no force or control.

I wasn't excited to go to this concert until the day came. I'm the type who reserves excitement, and it's not because I don't want to feel it—I just enjoy the present moment. Typically,

I just stay so far into the moment that I don't have the ability to get excited for future moments. I believe that's the key to my success, to my happiness. My personal joy, that drives me, is experienced daily because I live in the moment. I'm way too damn busy to think too far into the future. I run a business. I am a business. I'm a son. I'm a brother. I'm a lover. I'm also a taco connoisseur, and I take each one of these roles seriously.

That day we woke up right next to each other like every other day. Me, wearing my perfect six-pack abs that I've slaved for in the gym and in the kitchen, and her wearing booty shorts that leave the bottom cusp of her booty cheek to hang out underneath the fabric. I'm a slow riser. I take my time when I get up. I sat at the edge of the bed and muttered out something without really thinking about it, "Are you okay? I feel like today is going to be a good day."

"Yeah, babe, I'm okay, as long as you're here," she said.

The sun light fumbled its way through the blinds. I could feel the air conditioning graze my shoulder blades. I got up and walked over to the siege chair that had no arms. My backpack lay on the left side, a blunt on the right, and my Nike shoes directly in front. I sat down, lit up the blunt, and looked at her as she lay there.

"Do you want to hit this?" I said in a calm voice.

She hit it first.

"I have to go start my day. There's a lot for me to do before this concert."

"You're leaving already, babe? I'm off work today. I want to hang out," she said in questioning tone.

"I have work to do. I will see you tonight. See the day."

She understood that my time was important to me, and more importantly, she knew that I needed to be introverted during the day. She knew she was getting my attention all night, but in order for me to be the best me, I had to be away from her. I left after I planted a kiss on her cheek and headed toward the door.

twelve hours went by

I sent her a text: "Babe, be ready by five o'clock. I'll be picking you up then so we can head down to the arena."

Her: "Okay, I'll be ready."

It was 5:45, and I knew she wasn't ready. I told her five because she takes forever to get ready. We really didn't need to leave until six, but these are the types of tricks you have to learn when you deal with a modern woman. I called her at 5:25: "I'm on the way. Be ready to come outside."

Then I hung up as soon as she said okay. Women like to sit and talk on the phone, and they relay a lot of emotion, information, and dialogue. She's a talker, and I had no desire to sit on the phone with her, especially since I was driving to her. I pulled up playing reggae music. I looked over to her seat to make sure it was clean and comfortable. I turned the music down because I didn't want to disturb the neighbors. Instead of calling and telling her I was there, I wanted to put more effort in. I walked up the stairs, walked into her apartment, and found her fully dressed, minus her shoes.

"Hey, babe. I just have to put my sh—"

I put my lips on hers and kissed her. For whatever reason, I did not want to hear her speak until she was dressed and in my car. This story is humorous to me. It's funny because she likes the order that I bring to her. She likes the tough-guy macho stuff, and it's just my most natural state. I've always been a leader, so to lead a woman feels natural for me.

I walked down stairs and put on a song that I knew she would like coming down the stairs to. Everything is a production to me. The lighting matters, the songs matter, and the color scheme of the outfits matter. I'm an artist, and everything in life is inspiring to me, or at least it can be, and so I wanted to create the perfect scene for her.

As she came down the stairs, I gave her nothing but direct eye contact. She smiled, but all I did was admire her. When she got to the door, I grabbed her left hand, wrapped my hands around her waist, and pulled her in tight like the seal on a peanut butter jar. I kissed her on the lips. She bit mine. I guided her to the passenger seat and shut the door. I felt like I was falling deeper in love with her. There were feelings deep inside of me that were being sparked, and I couldn't fight it. I couldn't deny it. Words left me at that moment because it was something that I couldn't explain. I was confused like a hungry kid that sat at a table full of food, that displayed a sign that say, "Don't eat any of this."

By the time we got to the stadium, the vibe was set for us to have one hell of a night based on connection, vibrations, and soul-wrenching music that would unite two lovers like the adhesive on the back of an envelope as it was sealed.

"I love you."

"I love you."

The concert was going on for about an hour. The music was perfect. I was one Blue Moon in. She was one margarita in. We were vining perfectly. We didn't bother touching our cell phones. We were so far into the moment with each other. As we swayed back and forth with the music, I grabbed her around the small of her back. She put her arm around my midback area. I turned her body directly toward mine and away from the stage. I looked her directly into her eyes and said, "Kiss me."

She leaned in and kissed on my lips and started to pull back. I wanted more. I wanted her to know that out of the fourteen thousand people in that building, nobody mattered besides her and me. I said, "No, kiss me like it's the last time."

When I said this, something took over. She became a different beast. She pulled me in this time and locked every inch of her lips on mine. I could feel the energy transferring from her body to mine and then back to hers. It was an orgasmic life cycle that we gave each other in that moment, and it felt like it could never end. It was at this time that I fell deeper and deeper into the oasis of love land with her. As a man, I never thought that a moment like this was something I'd want or desire. She made it all possible with her rhythmic hips, sultry eyes, and heart of passion.

As Drake bounced around, stage fireworks went off, camera phones were flashing, and purple-and-pink lighting cascaded over the two us. We were the only ones there, kissing under the ambience of the live music. On that night, she fell a little bit harder for my antics. On that day, I realized I had a potential wife, a potential life partner, a friend, a lover, the woman that I'd been praying for. It was at this moment that I started to understand, that this is what real love was all about.

I knew that I was falling in love with you when I stopped walking, let go of your hand, and watched you walked into the sunlight. You looked back, but I told you to keep going. I just had to observe you. I just had to appreciate you. I had to fully stay in the moment. For the first time in my life, everything made sense.

—Sylvester McNutt III

Best Friend:

noun

noun: **best friend**; plural noun: **best friends**

1. a person's closest friend.

It's not about how many best friends you have—it's about how many people will call you a best friend. That is the biggest compliment of all. You're the type of person who has people's back, you go above and beyond, and you don't seek favors in return. You just give what you have, and that is your magic.

—**Real Friends**, *This Is What Real Love Feels Like*

What Is a Friend?

Really sit back and think about this. What is a best friend? What does it even mean to call someone a best friend? Before we go that deep, we should just explore the thought of "what is a friend?"

To be a friend, you simply need to share a bond and a mutual affection for each other. That's why we make so many friends throughout our life journeys. It's rather easy, and as long as you open your mouth once in a while you shouldn't struggle too much with it.

Friends can be people you talk to on the weekends when it's time to go out. They can be people you only see when you're at your gym. They can be the people you share a class with, even if you need talk outside of that class. Hell, a friend can be a person you bump into every few months and talk to for hours on end but don't see again until another three months go by. At the end of the day, a friend is someone who's like you, even if it's just for a few moments.

Friends have common bonds and can even come together through disagreement, through differences, and through dissonance. Hell, some friends enjoy each other because of the terror they cause each other. Sometimes athletes become great friends with each other simply because of the way they competed with each other. If you have friends, don't take them for granted, because as much as we explore the different levels of friendship, there are still people who feel as if they have no friends. I would beg to differ, because a friend is really just anyone who chooses to share energy with you. A total stranger is only a stranger until you know something about him or her. It only takes fifteen minutes over a good cup of coffee in order for us to tell each other our deepest secrets, and that makes us feel like we know each other. Well, maybe not coffee for some of you— maybe vodka or rum, but either way, the bonding can occur quickly.

Think back on your life. Think about the friendships you've had. Some that you wish you could feel again. Some you wish never happened.

All of them taught you something; they made you who you are. In fact, you're alive because of your friends. We have many other labels to use, such as brother, husband, or teammate, but these connections can all be summed up with one simple word: **friend**.

The Sporadic Friend

We all have this person in our life. It's a friendship that may have faded or may have never blossomed into the deepest connection, and both are okay and acceptable.

It's a friendship where you see or talk to each other sporadically, and never consistently. However, it's never appears to be lacking.

Last night I went out to opening night of the NFL. It was the Broncos versus the Panthers. A game that everyone wanted to see because it was a rematch of the Super Bowl.

My friend Julius and I had been in contact

a few days before the event. First through Snapchat, then through text, and then finally a quick call to confirm plans. I went home that night and talked to my girl about my friendship with him, and then I realized I was at the point of this book where I was writing about friendships. I told her, "Everyone needs a friendship like Julius and I have. I believe that we don't talk often, consistently, nor do we force each other to speak. Our friendship is amazing because even though we don't speak regularly, when we do speak we focus on giving each other the truest communication. We talk about controversial topics. We talk about our emotional welfare, as well as surface concepts too, like sports."

What I like about this type of connection is how we never pressure each other for anything, but we ultimately give each other everything when we do talk. If you have a friend like this, make sure you be mindful of the connection. It's important that we really evaluate what it means to be a *friend*. It's all subjective, but sometimes we look at friendships and expect that we can only have these immaculate best-friend connections, and that's false, because this type of friendship is actually common, especially in this busy world we have created.

In the world of "fake busy," I have an affinity for anyone who makes an effort to be in my life, to be there and to add value, even if it's just for a moment.

— Sylvester McNutt III

I Miss My Best Friend

I miss my best friend. The old best friend I used to have, the one who used to go all out for me, the one who used to just "get me." I miss him because he was in my life at a time when I needed him. I was a little bit lost. Confused. I was a little fucked up, but he accepted me. He took me as I was and allowed me to live freely and comfortably, and this is why he'll always be a friend to me.

I wish we talked more. I wish it could back to how it was, but I understand that even great friends grow apart. It's just the way life is set up, and well, it sucks, but damn, do I miss him. I wish I could call him now, invite him over for pancakes and tacos, or maybe just one of the options.

I have to really think about this, because life isn't promised. If he's still alive, I should call him and say hello, even if it's only for a moment.

The worst feeling ever is sitting at someone's funeral wishing you could've done more, been better, or reached out more. That is the worst feeling in the world. Regret. Shame.

"One of the best feelings ever is being with someone who understands how to sit with each other in silence. A lot of people struggle with small talk, filler conversations, & talks about subjects that have no depth and no relevance. Sometimes, sitting with someone you love and talking about nothing is everything. Just the presence of each other is enough. That's a blessing that only real lovers can appreciate."

– Sylvester McNutt III

and that's the
crazy thing
about the word
friendship;
it has the word
~~END~~ inside it.
we want them to last,
but *some*
must end.

As life shifts and distorts, you want a warrior,
a fighter, a soldier to go to war with you.
The same person who heals you should be
the one you lie in bed with and watch silly
programing on Netflix. The tears that you
shed should be caught by a kindred soul
who cares to serve you in the same way
that you serve your lover. No pain. No trust issues.
No drama. Just dreams, and flights, and
memories of everything and nothing. Flights from
the land of confusion to the island of each other,
where everything makes sense and nothing costs
money. On an island of love with your best friend,
where the only thing you truly need is each other.
See, once you fall in love with your best friend,
that person become your family, your spouse, and
your counterpart for all of life's quests. When it
comes to love, always make sure the person who
sits across from you at the table is your best
friend. Be that for your lover too.

– Sylvester McNutt

It's real love when you feel like you can be yourself, when your lover laughs with you, and when you make each other feel as valuable as oxygen. And most importantly, when you can look over and say, "You are my better half, my purpose, and my heartbeat." You know that this is what real love feels like because this person is your best friend. A friend who gets you. Yes, this is real love because the idea of you two being separate just doesn't sound accurate. It's real love when you feel everything with each other so deep: the skin, the bones, the blood flowing through the body, the emotions that can't turn over into words, and the flesh that tingles when you to touch each other.

– Sylvester McNutt III

On Self-Care

"Self love is the ability to look at yourself in the mirror, with no judgment, the ability to observe every behavior you do, and to fully accept that report without any equivocations. Self-love is about observing yourself and then it is always about adding value to your life."

-Sylvester McNutt III

For the rest of your life you will have thousands of thoughts. Please make sure that all of those thoughts are as positive and as encouraging as possible. Honestly, the rest of the world is against you, you don't need to be against yourself. Speak kindly to yourself. Be forgiving to yourself. Be open to learning new versions of yourself because you'll never stay the same. Part of the growth process means being kind to yourself about who you used to be and even who you are, today. Be kind and accepting of who you are. You are deserving of the deepest levels of kindness.

-k i n d n e s s, Sylvester McNutt III

Self-Love Mindset

Growing up, we don't often hear the term *self-love*. Love is portrayed as something that occurs outside of us. After decades of finding and losing love inside of other people, I've determined that the only love worth chasing is self-love. Self-love allows you to attract a higher version of love from others. It allows you to put yourself in healthy, in smarter, and in more rewarding situations.

You'll always go broke, feel lost, and trapped when the only love you chase is from a person or entity that is outside of you. Understand and accept that at all times, true love does exist and is inside of you. Your mind may be clouded. You may be talking down to yourself. You may be grading yourself on someone else's scale of what acceptance is. Understand and accept that true love is always about acceptance and will never be about anything else.

Make a decision right now, and allow it to last forever. Allow that decision to be that you will always continue to seek a higher version of yourself, to accept that you will love yourself deeper and deeper every single day. Do this and understand that love is always about your actions and what you say to yourself. Speak positively to yourself, because the last thing you need is to tear yourself down with words. Words are too powerful to play with.

Mental Strategies to Implement Self-Love

Become aware of the perception of yourself that you accept. Many times, as adults we still take on the perception of ourselves given to us by our parents, by media, and by our peers that we idolize. It's safe to say your perception of self, through others' lenses, is going to always be slightly off. Become aware of how your parents see you, how your friends see you, and what society is telling you, and then consider accepting this thought: you are what you are, and what you are today is who you are. Your mission is to fully accept yourself, as you are, today.

Live in self-acceptance. You're probably guilty of it. I was at one point. It's okay. We all, at one point or another, have overguessed our abilities. We've sold ourselves on how great we were when it was just a stretched truth. It's okay—laugh about it, but don't live in denial of who you really are. Fully accept yourself as you are. This is a key component to self-love.

Stop taking the energy and attitudes of everyone around you. We take on so much energy by doing this. It's okay to reject energy that literally makes you feel sick, that literally makes you feel unworthy, or like you're just totally out of place. Reject the energy that doesn't make sense for you. It's not your job to take others' energy. It's your job to manage your own.

Behaviors to Implement Self-Love

Water is love. I can't stress enough how important it is to drink water, and not just when you get thirsty but at all times. If you really want to know what real love feels like, give yourself at least a gallon of water per day. They may sound like a lot if you're not doing it, but trust me, your body will thank you later. You need water to digest food, to repair cells, to clear acne, to lose weight, to have strength, to flush out toxins, to keep your body temperature regulated, and a myriad of other reasons. Always remember: water is love.

Daily meditation. Some people have this idea that meditation is the art of not thinking. I'm sorry if it was presented to you like that. That not what it is. I don't believe you can literally stop the process of thinking. However, what I have experienced through the practice of meditation is a suspension of thinking. Almost where you're not aware that you're thinking. Start by breathing deeply. Take at least ten deep breaths and calm your body. From there say positive things to yourself like, "I am healing" or "I am happy." You can say them aloud or just think them to yourself. Either way, that's meditation. Meditation is good to relieve stress and to let go of negative elements, and most importantly, it helps you connect with yourself, which is very important.

Consistent physical exercise. Some people have ideas of fitness that have nothing to do with them, and that's why they avoid it. Some people think that because you've been eating bad for a decade and have never worked out, you can't get in shape, and that mindset is egregious. Some people see a particular body type and think that they must achieve this body or that body. Again, this is egregious. Fitness is about strengthening your muscles, which supports your bones. Fitness is about working on your motor skills, about relieving stress. Ultimately, it's about an attempt to keep yourself alive longer, and that sounds like real love if you ask me.

Self-love is
real love.
If you have it,
protect it.
If you need it,
look within.

- Sylvester McNutt III

You are robbing yourself
of happiness and joy if you say
that you are broken.
You're not broken. In fact,
that is literally impossible.
You are overcoming.
You are in the state
of recovering from adversity.
If you can be broken, then please
assume that you can be healed,
because as humans,
we have that innate ability.
—*you're healing*, Sylvester McNutt III

at one point, I was broken and torn into a thousand pieces. i watched my heart, my soul, and my ability to love myself fall from the sky like confetti. the heartbreak i felt left the taste of blood on my teeth and the feeling of paralysis in my soul, and it left me angry. i cried tears that i'll never get back. i stayed up on nights when i should've been slept. here's the kicker—i've grown, and in some odd way, i appreciate everything that i went through. it taught me to be a little more patient, to be a little more understanding, but most importantly, it taught me that i'm as tough as they come. moving forward, i'll put myself first until i meet someone who is worthy of the blessings i bring. i've been broken, but i am not broke. i am exactly where i am supposed to be. a warrior, a fighter, a lover.

—Sylvester McNutt III, *This Is What Real Love Feels Like*

I'm forgiving everyone who has caused me pain and suffering. I no longer want to hold on to it. It does no good to be bitter, to be jaded, to hold on to anger from some time ago. My forgiveness is not attached to naivety. I forgive, and I move forward, but I'll never forget how certain people made me feel. My healing process is more important than appeasing people who only offer me pain. I forgive you, but stay away. Stay far away.

—*f o r g i v e n e s s*, Sylvester McNutt III

It's so simple now. I'm a good person, and I want to be in a relationship. I don't have the patience or desire to chase people who don't want to be caught by me. I don't have the time to play games about who should call whom and to investigate shitty behavior. I'm grown; I love hard. I give everything I have to my relationships. I'll invest time and genuine concern, and will use any available resources to make it work. I have to be with a person who wants it just as bad as I do.

—*It's simple now*, Sylvester McNutt III

Be Thankful for Your Ex...

Some of the exes we dated came from hell.
Some of us ARE the ex from hell.
Either way, be grateful because they
taught you how to be a better lover.
They also gave you awareness around
what you will and will not settle for.
Don't be mad at them for anything,
because it's not worth the energy.
Be grateful that another human
shared space with you, and move on.
Once you can truly appreciate and remain
grateful for the experience, you'll truly heal.

Don't ever think of your ex as an enemy,
as a past memory that is negative or
as if your ex somehow ruined your life.
That is the victim mind-set, and you are
giving that person power over you. Never, and
I mean ever, give your exes power that they
don't deserve. Your goal is to make them
powerless, and in order to do that, you're
going to require yourself
to forgive them. That's true healing.
That is how you know that you're moving on.
Forgive them so the negative energy that
Lives inside of you can vanish.
—*forgive your ex*, Sylvester McNutt III

Love for the Person You Hate: Forgiveness

If you hate your ex, you will always suffer. If you hate the person who caused you the most trauma in your life, you will always suffer. If you still hate the kid who bullied you in high school, you will suffer greatly. If you're still suffering over what happened to you as a kid, please accept that part of that is your choice. You are not responsible for what happened to you when you were a kid. You cannot go back and change any of that story. The only thing that you can alter is your perspective right now.

Now, don't take this poetry as a statement that mental health issues don't exist. My friend, I've felt the trauma. I felt the depression. I've been at the bottom of the ocean without a mask. I'm on the same line and wave of life as you. Never above you and always with you. It does take time to heal, to patch up scars, and to exist in a new you.

However, no matter what I think, no matter what we've been through, FORGIVENESS is the most important path for us. Forgiveness allows us to heal. Forgiveness gives us everything we need to move on. Until we forgive, we will suffer, because we will hold on to hate, on to anger, and on to a consistent state of suffering. You no longer have to deal with that. Forgive yourself. Forgive them. Give love to everyone because they have taught you something. Even if there are people you hate. Give them love.

"you heal your soul when you choose
to forgive; it empowers you and allows
your consciousness to rise. you hurt
yourself further if you decide to allow
the pain and resentment to stay inside
of you. being mad at them keeps you
as a victim. victims have now power.
forgive. move forward so you can be in
a position of power. after you read
this, you can't forget it, and so the rest
is up to you. will you forgive, or will
you continue to make yourself suffer?"
  – sylvester mcnutt iii

Damn, we live in a generation full of people who brag about being coldhearted, love cutting people off, and are skilled at letting friends fade away.
—*fade,* Sylvester McNutt III

I'm not a fan of voids and people who like to come and go. Stay in my life, or stay gone. It's not optional, because my life isn't going to be used as a gateway drug to someone else that's more potent. Take me as I am. Look me in the eyes and see the soul that burns like a Miami summer day. If you choose to walk away from me, from my passion, from my dedication, it's okay, but there won't be chances later. That's not mean or cruel. I just have to protect myself from people who don't see my value.

 —*no fades*, Sylvester McNutt III

Healing is about letting go. Usually, we cause a state of suffering because we hold on to potential, to memories, or to other illusory feelings that keep us from a accepting the reality. True healing is about letting go of the sources of pain, letting go of the toxic mind-sets that hold us back, and must contain forgiveness. You have permission to forgive yourself and to forgive anyone that caused you pain, directly or indirectly.

—*letting go*, Sylvester McNutt III

The Woman I Will Marry

She had a rough day at work, again, and it's starting to take a toll on her. But she didn't want to talk about it. She liked to try to work through her problems. The last thing she wanted to do was bring me into her problems and drama. I could tell she had a lot on her mind. I wanted to alleviate it, but she was so damn stubborn. I poured her a shot, grabbed her hand, and hugged her like it was going to be the last time I held her. I said, "Baby, you don't have to tell me what's wrong. All you need to know is that I'm here for you, through it all, and that is my promise to you." A small tear came to her eye, and I wiped it before it fell. She smiled, and I felt it all start to release and leave her shoulders. She knew that everything was going to be okay. I smiled back as I looked her in the eye while clinching her tight and close. I never want to see her hold on to any pain, so whatever I can do to rid her of it, will be done. After we took our shots, she took a deep breath in and relaxed. She paused and really soaked in that moment. Although her pain came, I was able to help it go, and that's what she deserves from me.

The Woman I Will Marry

A few years ago, my best friend, William, asked me to write down what my wife was going to be like. He told me to keep it to myself. He said that doing this would actually help me attract my wife. Well, I wrote it down, and every woman I met after I wrote that was a spawn of Satan. Every single one of those women took a small piece of my soul and used me like I was carpet that was going to be discarded in a few days. They ran stampedes through my heart, had thunderstorms on my consciousness, and pulled at the strings of my lungs to try and take away my breath.

I had a horrible time dating. I felt like I was doing all of the right things, but I only met women who wanted sex and to Snapchat all day. One was with me every day for six months but wouldn't "commit," and when I told her that she was my girlfriend, she literally packed and moved to another state. I can't make that up. That's not poetry, and guess what—that happened twice. I fell in love with another girl who decided to move across the country. I had given up at that point. I never gave up hope—I just gave up effort, the search, and the energy needed to date. I literally told myself: focus on your business and leave these women alone. None of them want to build a kingdom. They just want to get popular on social media and text a bunch of lame-ass dudes who will never commit. I was a little bitter, but I walked away. I looked back at that letter one more time. I read it over and realized that the women I had just experienced were the ones I attracted. I had to realize that my morals were off, that my compass was off. I was pointing my energy in the wrong direction. I remember laughing as I drank a bottle of water at the park. I rewrote the letter.

Once I wrote the letter over, guess who walked into my life? The woman I am going to marry did. You walked in wearing black just like I thought you would. You wore a smile from ear to ear, just like I thought you would. You were a freak from day one, just like I thought you would be. You came into my life and had a desire to be my best friend. It felt like we knew each other from some prior life, some prior time, where we bonded and forged a universal friendship. I honestly feel like I meet you over and over in each lifetime, with a little bit different story, but it all ends the same: me and you together until the next life starts. I knew you were going to be my wife because you never made an excuse about coming to see me. You were driving forty-five minutes to come see me when I didn't even have a car. You wouldn't accept my gas money, because all you wanted was my time and my focus. I can honestly tell you, *This Is What Real Love Feels Like.*

If I'm being honest, I'm a sinner. I'm bad. I have a great heart, pure intentions, but I have a knack for messing up beautiful things. My only promise is that I'll be the excitement you've always craved, the danger that they tell you to avoid. I'll be the gentleman who holds the door and the savage that slaps you on the ass as you get in my car.

—Sylvester McNutt III

I'm the type of who will make you breakfast before work from time to time. I'm the type of man who will text you hearts and cute stuff like "I'm thinking about you" while you're at work. I'm the type of man who will bring you Starbucks at school. I'm the type of man who will make you tap my leg for air as I'm choking you and stroking from behind. I'm the type of man who will cuddle with you after sex so you know that I love you too. I plan to be there during every phase of the day—I'm that type of man.

— Sylvester McNutt III

Be with a man that puts effort into the connection with you. Your man should be your biggest fan, your healer and your supporter. A good man will challenge you, he will make you better but most importantly he will accept you as you are. A solid man will do the best he can with what he has to build a life with you.

– Sylvester McNutt III

I can't promise that I'll always be the best lover possible to anyone. I have bad days, I have moods that come and go, and I make mistakes at times. I promise myself that I'll always be the type of person who will be accountable for my actions, the kind of person who will try to learn from mistakes, and most importantly, I'll give my partner the same type of understanding and acceptance too. I do love completely, I do give everything that I have. I can promise that I will wear my heart on my sleeves, regardless of my flaws or shortcomings.

—*honest lover,* Sylvester McNutt III

Real love exists in the kitchen too. Standing over a hot stove, cutting vegetables and fruits, and preparing a plate of nutrition is an act of love. Making food should never be taken for granted. Food is nutrition, which your cells need to live, to grow, to continue to give you strength. Real love is that person who makes sure you always eat well. Cherish their efforts to keep you fed. Be grateful for every single meal you eat. There are some who haven't eaten in days. There are some who have no idea when their next meal is coming. You get to share love over food, so live in gratitude for all of that experience.

—*foodie love*, Sylvester McNutt III

I'm welcoming of those
who want to be in my life;
I cherish them.
For those who
want to exit it, I'll get up,
open the door, and will hold
it until you've walked out.

—Sylvester McNutt III

No man should live in a place of pride when it comes to his woman. Pick the right woman so she can be seen as an extension of you, as the better half of you, as the part of you that needs the most affection. If you are the root, then she becomes the leaves that make your tree worth looking at. We mustn't see our women as beings outside of us, no. We must see our women as we see our heartbeats—in fact, separation is the cause of all conflict. When you find the right one, she becomes your flesh, your inspiration, and your muse. The woman is a divine goddess whose sole purpose is to be cherished. Yes, your woman deserves a pedestal to call her own, one she can build value around.

—*p e d e s t a l s*, Sylvester McNutt III

Even on your worst days, you have the sun, the moon, the stars, and those lovely beauty scars. You don't have to look far. You never have to tear yourself apart or press restart. To find a little love, all you have to do is play your part. You're already a lover with a big heart. Nobody can change your fears, make you leave, or wipe those tears off your sleeve. You wear your heart strong and proud like a flag that waves in the sky. So the next time you cry, understand that someone is crying with you, someone feels it like you do, and you're not a damn fool. The alarm has been pushed. You're not scared anymore, not shook. Look up at your soul floating above you. This is your page, your semicolon, and your book. Write the story however you want to. But just know that we need you and the universe loves you. You're a star to us all, so smile wide like the rainbow, and allow everything that you don't need to go away like the fall. You're never going to fall, but you'll crawl, and you'll stand, and you'll run toward the sun. You're just a silly human. Don't be so hard on yourself. Pick up the book of self-love off the bookshelf and say, "I love myself."
—*self-empowerment*, Sylvester McNutt III

I think about the nights that
I spent alone where nothing made
sense, all of my thoughts roamed.

I was comfortable with
myself, but I was lonely.
I was thinking that I wanted
another person there,
and that was it only.

Those thoughts were so phony.
I craved another, needed another,
and desired someone whom I could
smother.

Someone that I could count on
hour after hour, that I could
climb through life with like a
tower, one that can be sweet,
while I bring sour.

Human connection really makes me
come alive. I'll walk, fly, or
drive to love if that's what it
takes to thrive. I am human.
Love brings me to life.

– Sylvester McNutt III

she sat in her
booty shorts,
no bra.
i sat in my
sweatpants,
no shirt.
we laughed.
we smoked.
we did art.
no television,
no outsiders,
just our vibes
and art.

– art love,
Sylvester McNutt III

they keep asking
me about the
meaning of love.
the answer is
simple: her.
—*h e r*, Sylvester McNutt III

She said that she
wasn't sure if she
wanted to date me.

"Queen, my soul is
already in love with
yours. You can be unsure,
but it won't last.
My beating heart was
created for yours."
—*the woman I will marry*, Sylvester
McNutt III

It was 11:00 p.m.
We sat at the table,
talking, connecting.

"Babe, let's go get
a bottle of wine. You
down, or are you down?"
I said to her in confidence.

She smiled from ear
to ear and said, "I'm down.
Let's go."

I smiled, kissed her on the
forehead, and we vanished into
the night.
—*real love*, Sylvester McNutt III

Everything changes when
you reach that
point where you
start leaving your
toothbrush, where laundry
starts getting mixed in
with one another, & where
you start thinking about
sharing bills. That's
real love. That's the next
level that many people
aspire to get to.

—*sharing space,* Sylvester McNutt III

Love, never,
until you came,
and now, no words
can describe this
cosmic feeling that
you give me.
—*about you,* Sylvester McNutt III

Give her a reason to post some cute shit on Snapchat.

— Sylvester McNutt III

Embrace her naked body.
You have no idea what
mental blocks she may have
overcome to show you.
Like her photos online,
thirst under her comments,
take her on dates where
engagement is the key,
talk about the endless
possibilities of life,
deliver her sex as if every
time was the last time,
and watch her love you
like you're rock star.
   —*she will fall in love*,
   Sylvester McNutt III

I bring her flowers because she needs to know that when I'm at the store, and I see something beautiful, it makes me think of her. The only way to capture that moment was to get the flowers, hide them, and deliver them with a smile and a hug. I love getting her flowers because I love seeing her smile and hearing her laugh. So when she reaches out to me, I will reach out with one hand to pull her close. I will reach out with the other to hand her the flowers that she deserves.

— *h e r*, Sylvester McNutt III

"no, i reject the idea that i should conceal my passion, my desires, and my interests to love deeply. i am not a half-way type of lover. the only way i'm going to love is by going all in. if it doesn't work, fine, but i'd rather look like a fool by giving every ounce i have versus any other option."
— *all in,* sylvester mcnutt iii

it's deeper than the
physical body for me.
i can have sex with anyone
but that's not the only
mission. sex alone,
without the vibe is not
my lane or my
motivation. sex is
pleasure,
it's a connection to a
deeper version of
understanding someone.
before sex,
before the first kiss,
she has to feel my soul
deep inside of her. her
throat can't be the only
thing that's deep on her.
i need her mind invested
into me. i need her to
desire me way before and
forever after i touch her.
i'm after the deepest
levels of seduction
imaginable.
— *deep,* sylvester mcnutt iii

"and sometimes two souls
are in love way before
they meet each other
in the flesh."
– Sylvester McNutt III

And when she needs support,
I step up. If she has tears, I
wipe them. When she has fears,
I listen. If she needs mental
stimulation, then I put my
phone down, engage, and talk
to her. And when she does not
know how to express herself, I'll
listen to her soul. I show her the
attention that she needs so she
knows what real love feels like.
  —*attention*, Sylvester McNutt III

**To create a hit song,
this is what you need:**

You need a rock star,
great timing,
lyrics that touch the
heart, and a mood that
touches the soul.
You need the same thing to
fall in love too.
—*m a g i c,* sylvester mcnutt

ruining each other by
not being together:
she'll never find
another man to love her
like he did. he'll never
find another woman to
understand him like
she did; they need to
forgive each other and
move on, back to each
other. this strange love
they have can only exist
inside of the bond that
they have created.

—*soul mates who need to be together*,
Sylvester McNutt III

you're a hopeless romantic in society that shames love. that's why you're so damn passionate about attracting a love that lasts. you want raw passion, effort, and a soul that accepts you.

—*you're deep,* sylvester mcnutt

The hardest thing to do these days is find real depth inside of people. It feels as if people are proud to be shallow, to have weak connections, and to lack a true burning passion. I want it deep. I want it to untangle parts of my soul that have never been touched. I want to explore people with layers, like onions, like volumes. I want people to teach me things; I want people to allow me to give them new information. I need depth, where is it?

— Sylvester McNutt III

This is a little crazy to think about, but somebody is making their life better so they can be in a position to discover you, to find out what makes you spin, all because they want to create new memories with you.

—*attraction,* sylvester mcnutt

She smiled
every time
she saw him. It
was how she
said in a
nonverbal way,
"I love you."
—*real love*, Sylvester McNutt III

that man wants

to love you,

let him.

-sylvester mcnutt iii

sometimes,
there are no
second chances.

when love
comes, make
sure you're
ready.

never focus on
being perfect—
just focus on
being yourself,
focus on giving
everything that
you can.

you owe it to
yourself,

you owe it to
them.

– sylvester mcnutt

We can ask ourselves all we want what the definition of love is and how we can attract someone who will show that to us. We can believe that love at first sight isn't real. We can't give our exes power over us, and we can act like we can do it all on our own, **but all of that is a lie**. We are all tired of lying to ourselves, so let's be the dreamer in the middle of the classroom. **Let's not focus on being a savage but instead focus on being human.** Let's give each other love, in the form of hugs, handshakes, and good times. Love is inside of every single one of us, and this is what real love feels like.

—Love for self, humanity, and all

don't ever say that
real love doesn't
exist or that it is
impossible to reach.

you have to be love,
you have to attract it,
you have to manifest it.

– sylvester mcnutt iii

never search for real love outside of you.
it doesn't occur there.
real love, that kind that is sustainable
occurs inside of you, inside of your
brain, inside of your heart. when you
enter a relationship your goal should be
to find another person who is already
on a path of taking care of themselves. if
two people meet in a space, where both
is pumping life into each themselves, it
is easy to convert that energy at each
other. for real love, the kind of love that
poets write about, the kind that scholars
don't understand – look within.

-sylvester mcnutt iii

If you think that love is the reflection of what they do for you, then you have vastly misunderstood what love is, and you will suffer forever until you find the truth.

Love, is never about your ego. Love is about giving, love is about compassion. Love is about putting them first every single time, over and over, and over. Love is never about your petty desires. When you truly love someone all you want to do is put them on a pedestal and allow them to bathe in the attention, the affection, and the happiness that you feel they deserve. Love is not about you. If they give it back you're lucky. If you've found someone who wants to give you love too, then you're rich. Love is never about entitlement, ownership, or ego. Get your perspective right so you can give abundance. Once you live in the lane of giving abundance it becomes almost automatic that you will attract a lover who wants to give you abundance. If you stay in ego, then you will suffer – the choice is yours.

This Is What Real Love Feels Like.

-Sylvester McNutt III